How to Find a Profitable Blog Topic Idea

How to Blog and Generate Profitable Blog Topic Ideas (Better Blog Booklets)

By:
James Stevens

Published by Shepal Publishing,

All Rights Reserved,

Copyright 2016, New York

Table of Contents

Introduction 3

Chapter 1: Getting Started in Choosing a Blog Topic 5

Chapter 2: Choosing a Blogging Niche.................................... 9

Chapter 3: Choosing a Blogging Platform............................ 14

Chapter 4: Reasons Why Some Blog Niches are Non-Profitable 19

Chapter 5: Choosing a Profitable Blog Niche........................ 22

Chapter 5: Making Money with a Blog.................................. 26

Conclusion 29

Introduction

There are many people that do not enjoy employment, and are looking for alternative ways that they can make some funds. One method that is quickly gaining traction is blogging, as all that you basically need is a great idea and a computer. If you are interested in exploring blogging as a way that you can make some revenue, then you need to start at the very beginning. The best way is to come up with an idea that is bound to drive people to your website and thus elevate your potential to earn some revenue.

This book starts you on that journey. To begin with, you will get an idea of how you can come up with a topic that is bound to elevate your total profit. This is followed by discovering your blogging niche. If you want to come up with a profitable blog topic idea, you need to select a niche that will help you focus your ideas,

To monetize your efforts, you also need the advantage of an excellent platform for your blog, one that will give it a brilliant layout that attracts the attention of readers. With the right platform, you will also be able to make the most of advertising and similar options to attract even more revenue.

An awareness of blog niches that will not bring you a profit should be evaluated, as this will help prevent you from making a mistake. You will find that it becomes easier to make the right choices when you are aware of the pitfalls that you need to avoid.

This is followed by how you can create a profitable blog niche for yourself, so that the topic ideas you come up with are better able to result in conversions and clicks for your website. Finally, this book addresses what you need to do in order to make some money while you are blogging. Knowing all the avenues that you can take will ensure that you exploit the available opportunities so that you can make profit.

Read on, and discover the simple steps and choices that you can make to create a profitably blog topic idea and learn some key insights on what it means to blog.

Chapter 1:
Getting Started in Choosing a Blog Topic

Blogging is a new way that many people are exploring as a source of income. Just take a moment to pay attention to what is happening online and on television and without a doubt, you will come across information on bloggers. Bloggers basically feed the world with information, in way that is easy to understand and highly entertaining. People tend to believe more in blogs than they do in news outlets or more official channels.

This has led to an explosion of blogs in the past few years, with everyone trying to find a platform where they can share their voice. In addition, this has opened up the world of blogging to businesses that are capitalizing on the followers of these blogs, as a ready market. What this has meant for bloggers is money.

In order for this money to made, it is necessary to drive people to the blog so that they can click on the pages and interact with the information. The more clicks one has, the more profit they are able to make. Getting the clicks is best done by having a topic that will pull people to the blog. These types of topics are sometimes referred to as click bait, because they bait and hook the readers who feel as though they have to click on a link to get the information that they need.

As you consider the best topic, you can use the following guide to help guarantee your success. Try out the following: -

1. **Have a direction for your blog**

    Think about what you are hoping to achieve as you write your blog post or article. Are you looking to entertain your reader? Do you want to write a blog that will bring you fame? Is it essential that you create a connection? Whatever your reason may be, you should realize that you can monetize it to get a profit, as you tap into the specific market that is looking for the information that you are providing. Remember, that excellent content is key to making profit. So as you come up with the idea, work backwards, considering the content first and then creating a topic that will do your content justice.

2. Scour some blogs

You probably read lots of blogs yourself, so you know which ones have the pull that you are looking to achieve for your own blog. Evaluate those blogs, and discover which types of topics you find most appealing. When you are working on your profitably blog topic idea, you should focus on one that is related to what you like to read.

3. Check out Amazon

Amazon is a website that has huge potential in helping you discover which blog idea could actually bring you a sizeable profit. Before you get writing, do some research by looking at the list of bestselling books that are available on the site. What you want to take note of is the titles and subtitles of these books. If you choose a blog title that is similar to these, you are sure to attract attention of readers to your website.

4. Do not settle for one

As you are working on your topic idea, you will find that your mind jumps from one place to another, and you get a range of ideas. While you are coming up with your final idea, you should never discount anything that is passing through your mind. Instead, you need to take some time and write down all the ideas that are coming to you. As you do so, you will be able to evaluate what the advantages and disadvantages of each idea is. This can be done by simply assigning each option a weight. When you have done so, you should finish up with a list of top three.

Before you make your final choice of the three, do some research on other blogs that have topics that are similar. From this, look to see (or try and find out) which of these topics made the most revenue.

5. Provide a Solution

If you want a blog topic that will not fail you, make sure that you choose one which offers a solution to a problem. When a reader sees that your article or post is likely to fulfill a need that they may have, they will have a stronger desire to get them to click on your topic.

6. Enjoy What you are Writing About

In order for you to find a profitable blog topic idea, you need to be able to enjoy everything that you are writing about. This comes back to having the right content. When you enjoy what you are writing about, you will find that the content which you produce is much richer. In addition, you will also discover that you can be more creative, and come up with a topic that is sure to thrill your readers. When your readers are happy, then you will find it easier for you to make a profit.

When you are looking at creating a new topic for your blog that will bring you profit, you do not need to do everything that is necessary to reinvent the wheel. When you have a topic that is totally new, you will find it a challenge to get the right audience to make it profitably. You can use other blogs to 'copy' topics, in regards to getting the inspiration and information that yoou need, but you should also ensure that you create content that is different and which will set you apart from all the rest.

In addition, you do not need to focus on achieving perfection with your blog. Rather, you should ensure that your topic looks at progress and how you can lead more people to your website.

Rather than just spewing out content, ensure that your blog topic introduces a story, one that has twists and turns which will captivate your reader. Look at the big topic, and then try and find your niche. Once you do, it will be easier for you to make your topic able to generate the revenue that you need.

Chapter 2:
Choosing a Blogging Niche

If you have already considered starting a blog, you should be able to decide what your blog will be all about. When you have this type of direction, it will help you to come up with a blog topic idea that is sure to drive sales, revenue and profit. Many people start blogging about anything and everything that come to their mind; this is not a bad idea but the success of these kinds of blogs is always limited. If you want to succeed as a blogger, you have to set the limits and come up with a blogging niche that you will always stick to. You need to have an idea of what you like to write about, and a clear direction of what you want to focus on.

The reason why many people read blogs is because they want to find solutions to some of the issues they face in their everyday life, or for pure entertainment. Your readers should be able to get what they are looking for and something extra, which will be hard to get if you are jumping from one topic to the other. If you want to solve problems for your readers, choose a specific topic and deal with only that and they will be happy with what you are offering to them. This is the reason why niche blogs are becoming quite popular today. There are fashion blogs for instance which will help you stay updated on the fashion trends and what to watch out for in the near future. If you are interested in business matters on the other hand, there are financial blogs that you can always count on for any information and advice that you want at any given time. You will always go back to the same blogs because you are sure that they have just what you are looking for. There are entertainment blogs as well, which deal with entertainment and nothing more or less. These blogs will keep you entertained for as long as you will need it.

In as much as a niche blog will slim down your readers, it will at least keep them coming back and this is the most important thing for any successful blogger. The success of a blog is not measured by how many people have read a certain article but by how many people follow the blog to the end, which is why you need to choose a good niche for your blog.

Here are important tips that will help you find the right niche for your blog:

1. Choose to write what you know and love

One rule of the thumb for any blogger is to write what they are passionate about, and this means that you need to have a good knowledge about what you write and it should be something that you love so that you can bring it out in a way that your readers will love. Bloggers need to know that it is really hard to write about something that you have little or no knowledge about. It will come out in your writing and your readers will not be impressed.

When you write about the things that you love and topics that you understand the best, you will be able to put so much time and effort to it and this is what leads to the success of a blog. Ideas will always flow and this makes it hard for you to abandon your blog in the future. Another important thing to note is that you will never run out of ideas, and this is what will keep your blog up and running for a very long time. You can figure out how to monetize your idea by looking at other successful blogs that have written on something similar and figuring out what the twist is that they have taken.

Your readers will feel how passionate you are in the way that you write and this is what connects you to them. People will want to read something that has been written with a lot of passion. This will get you more followers than you had anticipated.

Choosing the right topic is therefore very important. You will not run into burnout or get dissatisfied at one time in life. Many bloggers make the mistake of considering profits more than their passion and they end up losing readers because they are not writing about things that they really know.

But how do you find that passion? This is not an easy thing for any writers. One would wake up one day and think that they know so much about a certain topic and after only a few articles, they realize that they have already run out of ideas. Good thing is that you can always find your passion, something that interests you deep within and that which will always be your favorite. There are different ways through which you can arrive at your passion:

- Through finding your hobbies- if you know what your hobbies are, you can easily tell the kinds of things that interest you in life and through that, you can find a passionate topic to blog about.

- Through the way you spend your free time- the things you do when you are free are the things that you are passionate about. These should direct you to some of the topics that will interest you for a long time.

- Through that one topic or topics you can talk so much about, even for hours, when you are with your family and/or friends

- Through the kinds of subjects that you loved so much way back in school or college

- Through what you love reading about

- Through the topics that you would love learning about

- Through finding out that one thing that you can be happy doing even in the absence of a pay

The reason why this is important is in order to avoid starting a blog that you might come to abandon later on. Once you start writing your posts, evaluate whether you are still enthusiastic about the topic from time to time in order to be sure that you are on the right track. It will be very easy to profit from a blog that is successful.

2. Find a Void in the Market

There are so many blogs in the internet today and if you go through most of them, you might come to the conclusion that every topic out there in life has already been covered. Bloggers should be prepared for this. Even if you want to pick out the most unique topic you should know that there is a high chance that so many bloggers have already tackled that topic. However, you need to know that there is a chance that not everything pertaining to that topic has been tackled. This is your chance to benefit from that particular topic.

You can for instance go through those different blogs and establish the right audience who are not given the right attention and purpose to give them what they are in need of. Find out what your target is and think of different ways through which you can satisfy their needs through your blog.

Find out what other writers have written about your target and focus on those whose needs have not been fully met.

You can also consider focusing on a particular geographical area instead of focusing on the general audience. This way, you will get deeper into helping your target identify with some of the things that are very close to them. This may not get you so many readers but it will give you readers who will keep coming back to read and learn some more.

Chapter 3:
Choosing a Blogging Platform

Before you even start thinking about getting started in blogging, blogging seems a very easy thing maybe because so many bloggers have been successful in it. This should not be different for you though and one thing that will make you a success is if you take time to think through each and every decision that you make. The last thing anyone wants is to spend so much money starting a blog that will not get off the ground. One of the most important things you should think carefully about is the blogging platform that you should go for.

Today, there are several blogging platforms that are available. When you go to these platforms, you will be able to make choices about your formats and layouts, choose different colors, and find creative direction that has already been conceptualized for you. This is the hardest part of blogging. Once you have this sorted out, it will become easier for you to highlight any great blog topic ideas that you have. You have to go through each of them in order to make a good choice on the one that you feel is right for you:

1. WordPress.com

This is the most popular blogging platform available today and good thing is that it is free of any charges. The platform will store your blog site's content for free. However, this can mean that you are limited as to the amount of features and services that you can enjoy in this platform. It is however a choice of many bloggers who do it out of fun and they do not want to invest any money in blogging. You can always start here then later on upgrade to a self-hosted WordPress blog where you can access more features and more services.

The advantage you get with WordPress is that you will not pay anything for setting your blog up and it is a very simple and easy to use platform even for those who have little or no coding knowledge. You will also get to choose from so many themes.

However, if you want a more professional look on your blog, you might have to go for a different platform or to upgrade your free WordPress version. You will also not have direct control over your blog and this means no control over any advertisements. The other disadvantage is that your site can be suspended any minute, without any prior notice.

2. Blogger

This is a free blogging platform that is owned by Google. With it, you will be able to access all Google tools for instance Analytics and AdSense therefore you can place AdSense adverts on your site. This platform is meant for bloggers who are in it for fun too; that is those bloggers who do not want to invest money in it but they want to enjoy some monetary benefits that come with the advertisements. It is a very easy to use platform, making it a great choice for beginners. With Blogger, you will have full access to HTML code, therefore you can customize your blog the much you want. The problem with Blogger is that you do not get to enjoy a large storage space and it does not come with a good number of themes that you can chose from. Your blog will also have a. BlogSpot on its title.

3. Wix

If you are a business blogger, Wix is a good choice of platform to go for. It has amazing capabilities that a blogger will need for instance ecommerce functions. It is for instance a perfect platform through which you can build your ecommerce business website but you will not have full control over your online shop. Some of the benefits you will get to enjoy with Wix are:

- Limitless bandwidth

- storage of up to 20 GB

- Ads are integrated

- access to options for domain registration

- It is very easy to use

- so many professional templates to choose from

Wix is very expensive though and some of the ecommerce tools that you will get here are not really advanced. You will also not be able to customize your site to your liking because of limitations.

4. WordPress.org

This is a different platform from the two above because it is a self-hosted WordPress platform. It uses WordPress software on a third-party server. With this platform, you can edit your HTML code, install plugins, and so much more because you have total control over your website and at the same time making it more professional. Many bloggers prefer a self-hosted platform, and it is in most cases the best choice to make but you have to be willing to invest some money into it every month. This is the best platform for business people, website designers and bloggers who want to get more out of their blogging site. There are so many benefits you enjoy with WordPress.org, some of which are:

- it is user friendly

- you have full control over your site

- more options that are search engine friendly

- you can customize your site however much you want

- you have access to more than 1500 themes and more than 2000 free plugins

You will however need to have some technical knowledge since you will be hosting your site on a third-party server. Good thing though is that there are hosts that offer immense support to help you with anything that you will need.

The other issue you might face is in terms of insecurity considering how popular WordPress.org is becoming these days.

5. Tumblr

This is another easy to use platform that is also very sociable, although it is designed for bloggers who like reblogging posts. If you are planning to venture into microblogging, this might be a good platform to consider but if you want to start creating long-form content or your readers, you might have to look for a different platform.

The benefits you will enjoy with Tumblr are many though for instance you have access to unlimited storage, you have access to more than 1000 themes and you can easily use CSS and HTML in order to customize your blog to suit your needs.

However, it will not be easy to back up your blog. You will also experience some problem trying to import your content form other platforms. There are just a few plugins too.

If you are just getting started or you are into blogging for the fun of it, you can pick any of the free platforms. The paid platforms are usually perfect for people who are in business. The best choice is the one that will give your site the functionality that you want.

Chapter 4:
Reasons Why Some Blog Niches are Non-Profitable

Bloggers are all over the internet these days and they are blogging just about anything that comes in their mind. This is a good thing but as an upcoming blogger, you should know that there are those blog niches which are profitable and these are the ones you should be focusing on. There are those blog niches which are totally non-profitable. There are so many reason out there why some blog niches are not profitable and some of these blog niches will never make it to the success point. There are equally many reasons why some blog niches are doing better than the others. You need to know all this so that you will be able to make the right choice of a niche to blog about if you are aiming for the profits. Here are some of the reasons:

1. Competition

Just like everywhere else, there is high competition over the internet especially if you are blogging about a topic that has already been exhausted by other bloggers. If you are blogging about a topic that has already been covered especially by expert, your blog is likely to fail. This happens mostly to bloggers who write about topics they know little about or common topics that everyone knows so much about.

It is important to find out just how much has been covered in other blogs before you think about writing a blog about a certain niche. One of the things you should always aim for is to get a good ranking in the search engines, which will be hard if you are writing about a popular topic over the internet. Unless you are an expert in a certain niche, it is good to stay away from topics that have already been well covered.

2. Expiration of content

This is another good reason why some blog niches are not profitable. There are bloggers who write about topics that will expire after sometime and after that time, the blog will not have any meaning to readers. If you write about sports for instance, or news or even about entertainment, you will have to try and remain relevant otherwise your blog will become irrelevant after sometime and his will deny you a chance to enjoy some profits through it. These are niches that suit experts so much because they can pay for a high valued content in order to remain relevant for their readers.

3. Periodic niches

These are niches about things that happen once or only twice a year. These may not be profitable. If you are blogging about Christmas for instance or about Easter, you should know that these are events that only happen once every year. Blogging on these kinds of niches will be seasonal too and this means that profits will only come through when you are blogging, which is regularly. If you want to enjoy profit through your blogging, blog about things that happen round the year and not just for a season.

4. Lack of adverts

There are some blog niches which make it hard for anyone to advertise their products or services in and these are the types of niches which rarely make any profits. If you are blogging about porn for instance or topics that are only suited for certain kinds of people, you may not attract any or many advertisers and this will make it hard for you to enjoy some profits for your blog site. It is therefore important to consider the kind of target audience you are writing to because if they are undesirable, or you are writing about something that a lot of people despise, you might end up with no ads on your blog site and hence little or no profits.

5. Banned topics

There are so many banned topics that people still blog about and this explains why their blogs are not successful. Drugs for instance are prohibited all over the world and all search engines would not want to feature such topics on their platforms. You will therefore be unsuccessful if you tried to blog about such topic. Consider topics like gang-life, something that is illegal in all countries across the globe. You will not even find anything about that over the internet.

Chapter 5:
Choosing a Profitable Blog Niche

Now that you know the kind of blog niches you should avoid for a profitable venture, it is time to see the kinds of blog niches you should be going for in order to enjoy full benefits that blogging brings. The question you should be asking yourself is just how you can find a profitable blog niche. This is because within the profitable niche, you can find an idea which will move your money to the next level. If you are a frequent blog reader, you can tell a successful blog by the number of readers it attracts and also the kind of content the blogger posts but it is not easy to know if it is a profitable blog or not. That is why you need to take enough time to conduct a thorough research in order to find a profitable blogging niche that you should go for. Here are a few tips that will make this search easier and fruitful:

1. Target the top bloggers

The first thing you should think about are the bloggers who make good money out of their blog sites. Find out what they write about, their blogging style, where they started and the efforts they have put in order to get to where they are. Note than you are not doing this in order to copy what they do but to get an idea of how you are going to do on your blog in order to enjoy their kind of success. It is easy to get a list of top earning blogs in the internet, therefore go through a few of them and learn something that will benefit your blog.

2. Search through a niche that you know

You are better off blogging about a subject that is familiar to you and a topic that you know so much about, therefore this should be a good starting point as well. What you need to do is to find out some of the topics that have been covered in an area of your expertise and how the best bloggers in that niche are doing it in order to enjoy the success they are enjoying. Find out how profitable blogs in that niche are so that you will know if you are eying a good niche or one that will not get you any profits. While searching through your preferred niche, check out the blogging style that your target audience love and the gap that you can fill in so as to know if it will give you what you are looking for or not.

3. Go for a niche that has a marketable audience

One of the most important considerations one should make in choosing a blog niche is his target audience. These are the people who are likely to read your blog. If you want to profit from your blog, your target audience should be people who have a bank account, because you want to target people who can buy something. Remember that your blog will attract advertisers depending on the target audience that visit your blog. If for instance you want to write something that will benefit the young children below 10 years of age, how will they buy anything that will be advertised on your site? Advertisers may not be willing to advertise in such a site and this means that your site will not bring you profits. These are important things to think about.

4. Choose a niche that you love

Passion is what will keep you blogging for a very long time and this is what marks the success of a blog. One of the things that will earn you some money in blogging is your ability to keep blogging. Advertisers will definitely choose a site that has a high traffic, and your consistency in blogging is what will keep them coming back. Besides, it is always good to work on

23

something that you are passionate about because even if it will not be well paying, you will still enjoying blogging and this can yield good results for you in the future.

5. Choose a niche that is always relevant

There are topics that expire after a certain period of time like I mentioned in the previous chapter and there are those that are always shining and relevant throughout the year. The latter will be the best topic to go for if you want to make some profits through blogging. News will for instance keep people coming back only that you will face a high competition, which may limit your chances of getting some profits especially if that is not really your expertise. This type of niche will be a challenge too since you will have to work on your blog full time to ensure that your readers are well informed and also in order to keep your blog fresh at all times. There are other niches which also remain relevant for a long time yet they do not need constant updating. You should research well and these kinds of niches in order to make a choice that will keep you benefiting and blogging for a long time.

6. Consider a niche that has a service or a physical product

These are the things that will bring you some money in the end. You need to consider niches which have physical products or service that you can recommend for your readers. This can drive traffic to your site and at the same time you will have something to well to your readers directly or through recommendations. You will also be able to make money through the space left for ads and sales. If you are good in promoting a service or product, this should not be really hard for you.

7. Choose your audience on time and learn everything about them

There are people whom you can freely talk to, people you can identify with and people you feel have issues that you can easily address and these are the kinds of people who should make your target audience. The most important thing even before you start blogging is to identify the people you will be writing to. Get to know them more and you will know how to address the issue at hand. A mistake you can easily make is choosing a niche just because it is successful and searchable in the search engines. You choose a niche as per the kind of people you are targeting. In this case, you should consider the geographical location of your target audience, the gender, and their age among many other considerations that will give you the kind of readers that will also bring some profits to your blog.

Chapter 5:
Making Money with a Blog

If you are into blogging for the profits, it is important to know how you can make money so as to start blogging and enjoying the profits. Everyone wants to make some money after all, therefore it is time to start finding ways through which you can monetize your blog. What you should know is that there are so many ways through which a blogger can make money and any kind of blog can bring you some profits, whether you are blogging for mere fun or you are in business. Blogging is not a way to get rich quickly though but if you put everything in order and you make the right choices, you can make enough money. Here are some of the ways through which you can make some money through blogging:

1. Use of ads- This is the most popular way through which bloggers make money through their sites. Basically, there are two main types of Ads that you can use in order to generate some income as you blog:

   a) Pay per clock adverts, also called cost per click ads. These are banners that are placed on the content or the side bar. Every time a reader clicks on that Ad, you are paid.

   b) CPM ads are those kinds of Ads whereby you are paid a certain fixed amount of money depending on how many people have viewed your Ad.

   If you are using a blogging platform that offers Google AdSense network, you will find benefiting from the Ads much easier. You will only be required to place a banner on your blog then AdSense will choose the right types of Ads that match your kind of blog and readers. There are other types of programs that work the same as AdSense, therefore you have choices to make depending on the kind of platform you are using.

2. Use of private Ads- These are a little different from the Ads I have mentioned above in that you will directly deal with business people and advertisers over the kinds of Ads they want you to place on your blog site. This is very easy with blog sites that are successful because so many people visit such blogs. In that case, advertisers will contact you for a chance to advertise on your blog page. Good thing with private Ads is that you will be the one to determine your Ad rates and the kind of Ads that will be posted on your blog page.

   Selling private Ads can take different forms, which are for instance use of buttons, banners and links. You can also opt to write something about a product or service or even provide a review on your blog. You can also use the advertiser as a promoter for your content, mentioning him at the end of your posts the ideas are many, therefore you choose the one that suits your best, then you can come up with a mode for charging for the advertisements.

3. Sell digital products- For bloggers who are not comfortable advertising other people's products or services on their blogs, you can always consider selling digital products that can generate you some income. Some of these products are for instance eBooks, apps, themes, plugins, music, videos, images, online workshops or courses among many others. Just ensure that everything that you sell on your blog site will be

27

beneficial to the kind of readers that visit your page since they are the ones who will be buying the products.

4. Use of affiliate links- Affiliate links can be used in your content. Affiliate marketing is currently one of the most popular ways through which bloggers generate income through their blog pages. Here is how affiliate links work:-An advertiser advertising through your blog promises to pay you a certain commission if a buyer of his product or service comes from your blog. He gives you an affiliate link that will be used to ascertain whether the buyer used your link or not for buying. The affiliate link should be included on your blog page.

5. Using your blog site to build your reliability- This is something important that can earn you so money elsewhere, not necessarily directly through blogging. There are so many opportunities out there for making money and most of these opportunities require people who are credible. You can use your site to promote yourself in order to increase your chances of benefiting from such opportunities.

6. Using your blog to market your business- This is a sure way to generate some income through your blog. If you are in business, you can always use your blog as a content marketing tool to promote your business and acquire clients. Many business people are doing this already and they are reaping major benefits. You only need to come up with amazing and inspiring content that will drive your readers to your website. You can start selling through your blog if you are starting a business or you can create a blog and start promoting an already existing business. Either way, you will be making more sales than before.

Conclusion

Now you have all the tools that you need to find a blog idea that will drive you to profitability. It is important that you look at the identification of your blog topic in a holistic manner, taking into account how you will blog and where you will blog. Creating a profitable blog topic idea can be simple, if you have the right support system in place.

With this book, you have learned what you need to do to find a profitable blog topic by exploring what is happening with your favorite blogs. You do not need to come up with totally new ideas to make a profit. Instead, you should look at what is happening with your favorite blogs, and use them for inspiration to help you make great revenue.

Make sure that you choose the right niche so that you are able to make a profit. In addition, the right platform can be the difference between making money or not. Enjoy your journey to creating a blog that will drive revenue and bring up your bottom line.

Made in the USA
San Bernardino, CA
04 September 2016